Cultural Clothes

Contents

Written by Leonard Karauna

Introduction

Cultural clothes are clothes worn by people from all parts of the world. The clothes often represent a country, usually because they were common clothing in history. Sometimes cultural clothing is worn every day, but more often it is worn during special occasions, like festivals and celebrations.

The style of the clothing is determined by the climate of the country, the materials available to make clothing, and ethnic traditions.

Sari from India

Kimono from Japan

Kilt from Scotland

Bunad from Norway

Chogori from Korea

Huipil from Guatemala

Piupiu from New Zealand

Sari
(sar ee)

A type of dress worn by women in India.

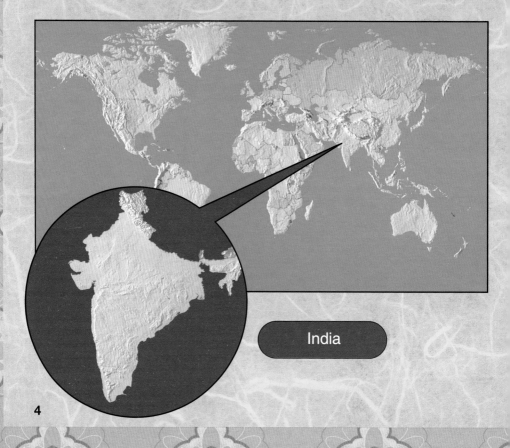

India

What a Sari Looks Like

A sari is made from one long piece of cloth that can vary in length from 13–26 feet (4–8 m) long. It is made of light fabric, with different patterns and shades for different regions of India.

The sari is draped around the woman's body, and tucked into the top of a long skirt. The long loose end of the sari, the *pallu*, is draped over the left shoulder and knotted at the waist.

A blouse, or *choli*, is worn under the sari.

pallu

choli

sari

pattern

petticoat

A petticoat and a choli are worn under the sari. The pallu is draped over the left shoulder.

Other Clothes and Adornments

Unmarried women and young girls often wear long, loose trousers called *salwar,* and a long blouse called a *kameez*.

Young girls often wear very bright clothes.

Men wear a *dhoti*, which is a long, white cloth wrapped around the waist. When the men work, the dhoti is wrapped between their legs, and looks like baggy trousers.

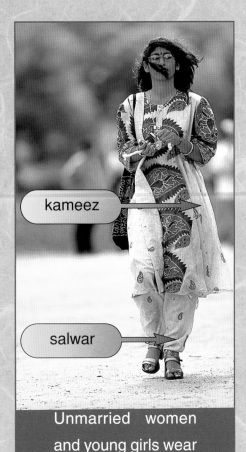

kameez

salwar

Unmarried women and young girls wear salwar and a kameez.

dhoti

Men wear a dhoti.

When a Sari Is Worn

Sometimes a sari is worn only at festivals and celebrations. A sari for these occasions tends to be longer and covers more of the woman's body.

However, the sari is also worn every day by some Indian women. The sari worn by a working woman in a factory is usually shorter and covers less of the woman's body. This makes it easier for her to move and is safer around machines.

Differences between a Sari for Work and a Sari for Special Occasions	
Sari worn for work	Sari worn for special occasions
shorter	longer
easy to move about in	not so easy to move about in
safe around machinery	not so safe around machinery

Kimono

(key mo no)

A long, loose robe, with wide sleeves, that is tied with a sash. A kimono is worn by Japanese men and women.

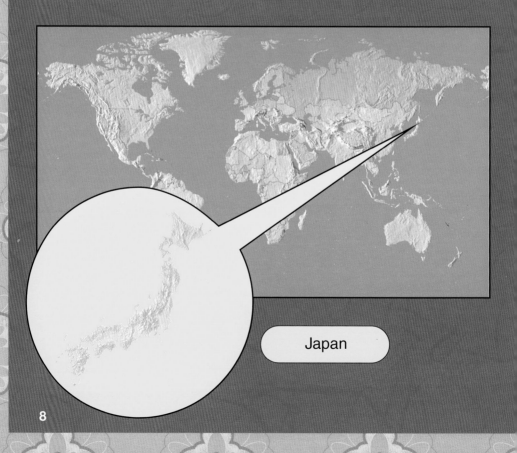

Japan

What a Kimono Looks Like

A kimono can be made from silk, cotton, linen, wool, or synthetic fabrics. The woman's kimono is usually brighter than the man's. The kimono has no buttons, but is wrapped across the body and tied at the waist with a very long sash called an *obi*. The obi is usually made of stiff silk or satin with embroidery. A man's obi is shorter and thinner than a woman's.

There are many ways to tie the obi, and each way has a different meaning. By looking at the way a woman's obi is tied, you can tell if she is married.

kimono

obi

A kimono is tied at the waist with an obi.

Other Clothes and Adornments

Japanese socks called *tabi* and sandals called *zori* are worn with a kimono and obi.

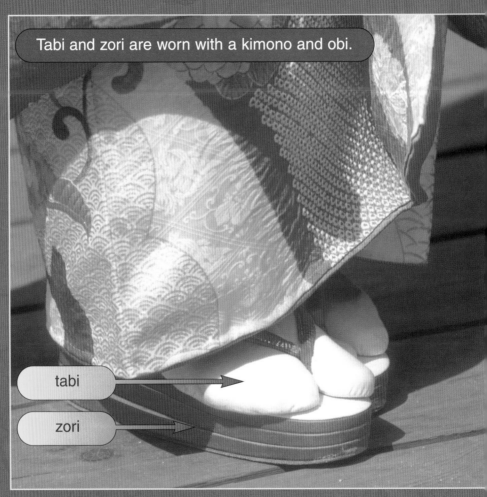

Tabi and zori are worn with a kimono and obi.

tabi

zori

When a Kimono Is Worn

A kimono is worn for special occasions, such as weddings, funerals, and graduations. A special white kimono is worn for weddings.

Many Japanese still wear a simple, comfortable kimono when they are at home.

A kimono can be worn for special occasions.

Kilt

(kilt)

A knee-length skirt made of pleated tartan cloth, traditionally worn by men in Scotland. A kilt is sometimes worn by women, too.

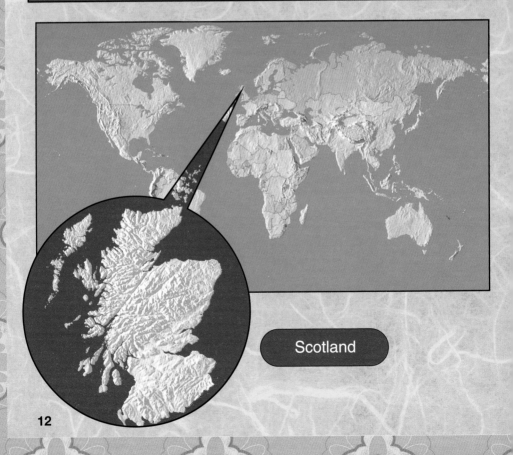

Scotland

12

What a Kilt Looks Like

A kilt has a checked pattern on it called *tartan*. The different tartans show which part of Scotland a person comes from or which clan they are part of.

A kilt is made from about 13–16 feet (4–5 m) of woven wool cloth. The first kilt was one long piece, wrapped around the waist, with the end brought up over the shoulder. But in the 1700s, it was separated into two pieces – the kilt, and a *plaid*, or *sash*, worn over the shoulder. A kilt lies flat across the front and is gathered in pleats at the back.

plaid

tartan

kilt

A plaid, or sash, is worn with a kilt.

Other Clothes and Adornments

A belt with a silver buckle is worn over the kilt.

Hanging down in front of the kilt is a *sporran*, which is a kind of purse. The sporran can be made from leather, sealskin, or even silver.

Knee-high socks can have a small dagger tucked into the side.

A jacket might be worn with certain tartans, and often the shirt beneath has a ruff of lace at the neck.

A kilt can be worn with a cap, a jacket, a belt, a sporran, socks, and a dagger.

The kilts of some clans are worn with a cap, called a *bonnet*, which bears the crest of the clan.

When a Kilt Is Worn

Some Scottish people still wear the kilt every day, but more often it is worn only on special occasions and for performances.

For evening dress, the woman wears a plaid, or sash, across her dress. The man wears a black dress jacket and black shoes with a kilt.

A kilt can be worn for performances.

Bunad

(boo nard)

A traditional dress worn by women throughout Norway.

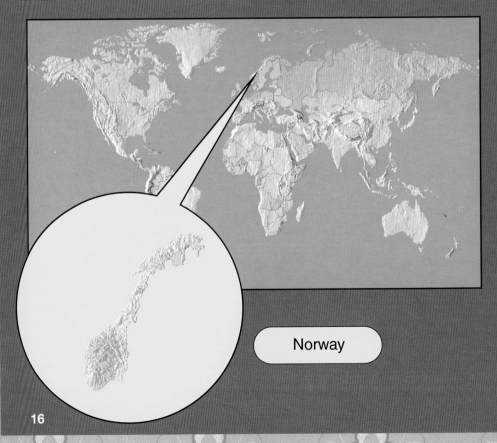

Norway

What a Bunad Looks Like

There are several parts to a bunad. There is a wool skirt, which can be short or long, black or white. At the bottom of the skirt are three stiff bands of material. There is also a wool bodice, which is usually red. This is embroidered with tiny white beads.

There are up to 200 kinds of bunad in Norway. The different kinds of bunad show what part of Norway the women come from.

wool bodice →

wool skirt →

A wool skirt and a bodice are part of the bunad.

Other Clothes and Adornments

Over the top of the skirt is a white apron. This apron has beautiful patterns on it.

It is important that black stockings and black shoes are worn with the bunad.

A silver brooch is worn at the neck, and often other gold and silver ornaments are worn around the neck as well.

Women might also wear a headdress. The headdress, or scarf, can identify a married woman from an unmarried woman.

An apron and a silver brooch are often worn with a bunad.

When a Bunad Is Worn

A bunad is mainly worn at celebrations such as Midsummer's Day. It is also worn at special events like weddings and festivals.

A bunad is usually worn at celebrations and special events.

Chogori
(jow gor ee)

A jacket that comes from Korea, and is worn by both men and women. People have worn this traditional clothing since 668 AD.

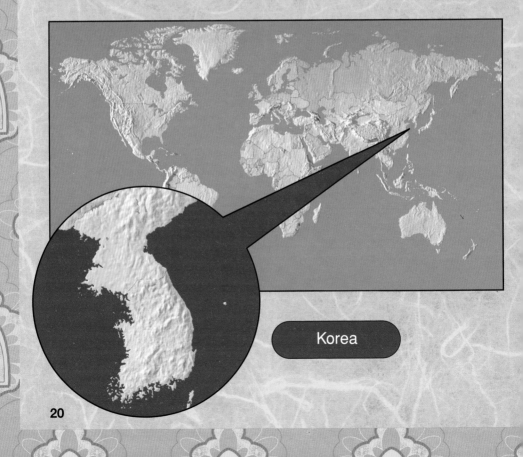

Korea

What a Chogori Looks Like

A chogori is like a short jacket. It is tied on the right side of the chest with a bright bow. The man's chogori is longer than the woman's.

The chogori can be made from hemp, cotton, muslin, satin, ramie, or silk. Cotton is used for everyday garments, and hemp for work clothes. Silk is used only for very special occasions. In colder areas, fur is added for warmth.

chogori

The man's chogori is longer than the woman's.

Other Clothes and Adornments

Women also wear a high-waisted skirt called a *ch'ima*. At the top of the ch'ima is a pleated waistband. This ties over the chest with long sashes. A *sok ch'ima* is an underdress worn beneath the skirt. Loose trousers are worn under the sok ch'ima.

Men wear white baggy trousers that are cuffed at the ankles, called *paji*, and a *turumagi*, or long overcoat. This can be worn by women, too. White socks are worn with flat, black shoes.

ch'ima

paji

black shoes

When a Chogori Is Worn

The chogori is worn at festivals and celebrations like New Year's Day or Chusok, which is Korea's Thanksgiving Day. The chogori is also worn at weddings and funerals. At a funeral, people wear traditional clothes that are mostly white.

The chogori is worn at festivals and celebrations.

Huipil

(we peel)

A kind of long blouse that is still the common traditional clothing among the Mayan women of Guatemala.

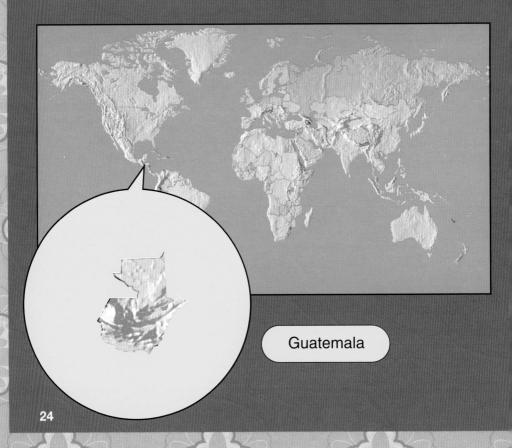

Guatemala

What a Huipil Looks Like

A woman wears a huipil, which varies in style for the region. The huipil is like a straight dress, and can be any length. It is usually made of wool or cotton.

The huipil is tucked into a long skirt that has been woven or embroidered in stripes and beautiful patterns. The patterns may be of birds, people, and geometric shapes.

In some areas, a short black apron can be worn over the skirt that the huipil tucks into.

huipil

long skirt

A huipil tucks into a long, patterned skirt.

Other Clothes and Adornments

A type of *poncho* may be worn over the huipil. The poncho also varies in style for the region, and can be worn by men, too.

Hats or turbans are worn. They are made from straw or felt. Some people wear jackets and sashes and carry bags.

People might wear shoes, or walk barefooted.

Men wear long, loose pants and long-sleeved, striped shirts.

Men can wear a hat with their striped shirts and pants.

When a Huipil Is Worn

Many people wear the huipil every day, and often for special occasions.

The huipil is worn every day by many people.

Piupiu

(pew pew)

A flax skirt worn by the Maori people of New Zealand for special occasions. Both men and women wear the piupiu.

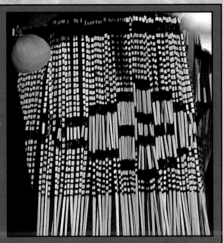

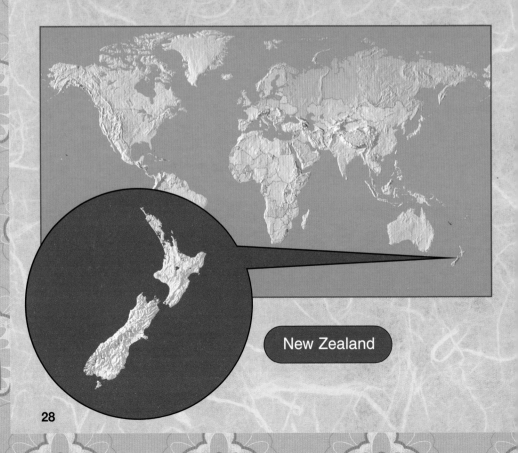

New Zealand

What a Piupiu Looks Like

The piupiu is a kind of skirt. Its length and style identify the person's tribe.

The piupiu is made from flax that has been treated and dyed. Long strands of dyed flax hang from a waistband. The flax is dyed yellow, and has patterns of black, and sometimes red, running down each strand.

waistband

piupiu

The piupiu is made of long, dyed strands of flax, which hang from a waistband.

Other Clothes and Adornments

Women wear a bodice called a *pari* and a headband called a *tipare*. The bodice and headband are woven with patterns that tell where a person comes from.

Men and women may wear a necklace carved from bone or greenstone.

A feather cloak, called a *korowai*, is worn by men and women of great importance at important events, like graduations.

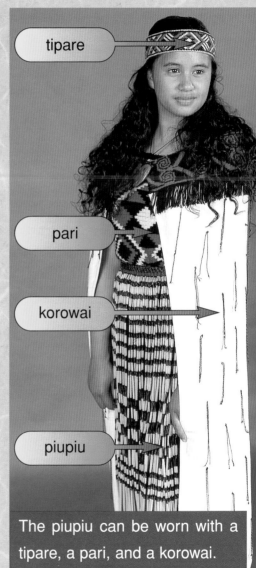

tipare

pari

korowai

piupiu

The piupiu can be worn with a tipare, a pari, and a korowai.

When a Piupiu Is Worn

The piupiu is worn only for special occasions and for performing Maori dances.

The piupiu is worn for performances.

Index